THE PURPOSE ADVANTAGE

How to Unlock New Ways of Doing Business

Jeff Fromm

Advantage Book Series

In each book, we highlight best practices and provide readers with practical tools for driving immediate organizational change. Our next book — *The Culture Advantage* — is based on research as well as the work Jimmy Keown and others on our team have done with leading brands.

Youth Culture

In 2010 & 2011, Jeff worked with The Boston Consulting Group to study Millennials as consumers. Since then, Jeff and his team have conducted dozens of research studies and written three best-selling marketing books that help readers move past the consumer myths and drive brand preference and sales growth.

Books available on Amazon
jefffromm.com | barkleyus.com | linkedin @jefffromm

I have the most amazing team anyone could hope to have. I could fill a separate book with thank you notes. I'll try to be brief.

To Sarah Jo Crawford who was instrumental in writing and editing, you are both wise and remarkably easy to work with. I strive to be as talented as you are if and when I finally grow up.

To Hannah Zimmerman, Jen Mazi, Mike Swenson, Sam Meers, Joe Sciara, Samantha Twenter and Jason Parks, I appreciate the guidance and thinking you provide on an ongoing basis. I know I have looked for input often without expressing enough gratitude. Thank you.

To Rohit, Marnie and the team at Vicara Publishing, thank you for the commitment and stewardship.

To Josh Bernoff, your comments made this book tighter. Shorter is always hard and I appreciate the insightful ideas. Your "no bullshit" approach to calling out some weak spots was appreciated.

To the team at Forrester including Jim Nail, Dipanjan Chatterjee and Bret Sanford-Chung, each of you made your time and insights available on calls as I did my homework on trends. Your thinking often inspires and informs me about the ever-changing preferences of modern consumers. Thank you each for being so generous with your ideas.

To Beth Perro-Jarvis and Mary Van Note, thank you for the ideas, suggestions and words of caution. Your comments pushed me to rethink aspects of the work.

GRATITUDES

To the Barkley Design & Experience team—Edwing Mendez, Hannah Lee, Joni Thomas, Skyler Schlageck, Arthur Cherry and Paul Corrigan—for your hard work crafting a thoughtful design with amazing illustrations.

To Brad Hanna, you started me on this journey with a simple question in 2010 around "How will Millennials impact brands in the future?" Co-leading the first study with The Boston Consulting Group in 2010 and 2011 led to my first book, and the rest, as they say, is history.

To Jim Elms, you pushed me to go further and think differently. And it worked.

To my business partners at Barkley and FutureCast, you each give me the freedom to explore what drives consumer preference and look at the trends shaping our lives. Thank you all!

To my family, from my lovely wife Rhonda to my three wonderful adult kids, Laura, Abby and Scott. Thank you each for being wonderful.

To my parents, Bernie, Bill and Jackie, and my family, Andy and Laurie, Dan and Kristen, Eddie, Julie, Marti, Caroline, Leo, Lucy, Eli, Walter, Charlie and Joshua. Thank you all for making life more meaningful.

I leaned heavily on team members to create this book. The workshop portion is designed to allow you to leverage our past experience running brand purpose workshops. It will equip you to take immediate action to rethink why and how to operate in favor of values-driven consumers and values-driven employees.

Lindsey DeWitte

Lindsey is an integrated marketer dedicated to helping brands define, live and share their brand purpose. She leads a sought-after strategic communications practice focused on the development of reputation-building business and communications strategies.

Lindsey consults with global brands to uncover and elevate reputation-enhancing corporate initiatives, pull purpose back into the brand DNA and create campaigns that will mobilize internal and external audiences.

With communications expertise in everything from issues and crisis management to influencer relations, Lindsey is passionate about helping brands improve how they act, react to and engage with modern consumers.

Jennifer Cawley

Jennifer has spent two decades helping transform organizations through brand purpose and reputation management. Her work as a senior communication strategist has helped brands connect consumer insights into scalable purpose strategies.

These strategies span a wide swath from launching communications for the first major-scale, U.S.-based blockchain initiative for a protein brand, to leading a rebrand to future-proof an iconic yet struggling not-for-profit brand.

Jennifer excels at creative ideation and problem solving and has developed nationally award-winning strategies for consumer packaged goods, retail, restaurant, travel, lifestyle and non-profit clients.

Jimmy Keown

Jimmy is an experienced leader in both brand and internal culture strategy — and leads a practice dedicated to the discipline, methods and practices of "Brand Culture Thinking™." He helps clients deliver on the potential that brand purpose can offer across the entire workforce, and helps organization's build Brand Cultures that are aligned, focused and inspired to deliver on the brand's biggest possible opportunity. Jimmy and I are working on a book called *The Culture Advantage* which helps companies with Winning Inside to Win Outside™.

He helps executive clients navigate and enable the potential of purpose through internal Brand Culture and purpose strategies, actions, programs and communications with their internal stakeholders and employees.

Philippa Marshall Cross

For over 15 years, Philippa's passion has been helping global brands bring environmental and social impact into their core to engage with consumers around a shared purpose.

As Sustainable Business Director at Unilever, she developed sustainability programs for brands including Ben & Jerry's, Hellmann's and Knorr that delivered tangible business impact, including increasing consumer loyalty and earning additional shelf-space at retail. These brands, and others that form Unilever's Sustainable Living Brands Index, are growing twice as fast as other brands in the portfolio and fuel 70 percent of Unilever's total growth.

Philippa has a master's degree in Sustainability Leadership from the University of Cambridge and continues to be involved with the program, developing the next generation of sustainable business leaders. Philippa has lived in cities across Asia and Europe, but now calls Kansas home.

All trademarks and service marks appearing in this book are owned by their respective brand owners and are used solely for editorial and illustrative purposes. The author is not affiliated with, sponsored or endorsed by any of the brand owners.

"This book contains many brand examples as well as a workshop to help readers build their best possible brand purpose."

Dipanjan Chatterjee, Vice President and Principal Analyst, Forrester

"MOD Pizza was built on the principles outlined in *The Purpose Advantage*. We are changing lives, not just selling pizza."

Scott Svenson, CEO, MOD Pizza

"This book is a go-to guide for the journey to build a brand with a soul, one that deeply matters to people. Follow it authentically and your brand will outperform the competition."

Carol Cone, CEO, Carol Cone on Purpose

"For investors today, corporate responsibility and ESG are important factors when evaluating potential investments. This book is equal part inspiration and "how to" for brands seeking to create societal benefits for consumers and strong returns for investors."

Anton Nicholas, Partner, ICR

"Purpose-driven brands have an edge in building emotional connections that resonate more with people. This book is the go-to resource for creating a brand with a soul."

Marla Kaplowitz, CEO, American Association of Advertising Agencies

"*The Purpose Advantage* demystifies today's consumer decision making. Fromm brings research to life in a witty and approachable manner that blends real stories and data at the intersection of where purpose meets profits."

Bill Theofilou, Senior Managing Director, Customer Insights & Growth Strategy, Accenture Strategy

"Jeff and his team at Barkley understand that Purpose is not just a marketing initiative. Living purpose across the business is imperative for modern brands today."

Jill Cole, Chief Marketing Officer, Thrivent Student Resources

ONE

What Matters is What You Do Next

"How can I help you today?" A smiling, young employee waited to take my order as I puzzled over the options.

"Is it really the same price, no matter how much I put on it? Even if I add ALL the veggies?!" I asked.

"It really, really is. It's called a MOD pizza for a reason."

When I first heard about the pizza chain, I was sold on the idea of a custom pie, but truthfully, didn't expect much. However, within the first 60 seconds of my first MOD® experience, I knew something was different.

At first glance, the large wall by the people waiting in line reminded me more of a teenage bedroom and less of a retail chain. It was plastered with photos — image after image, each offering up a different smiling face, much like the one that greeted me at the counter. The wall to my left presented a graffiti-esque quote, "What matters most is what you do next." The letters M, O, and D stood out in bold, contrasting red.

MOD. There it was again. A MOD pizza? According to the menu in hand, a MOD pizza was an 11-inch pizza, crafted right in front of you. A scan of the menu listed unexpectedly named topping configurations — Jasper, Calexico, and Dillion James — or 30 craveable toppings to make your perfect pizza. Guaranteed, according to a short paragraph at the end.

"Don't love what you ordered? Let us know. We're all about second chances."

Second chances. I pondered this as I watched my pepperoni, spicy sausage, mozzarella and rosemary pizza slide into a flaming oven — I clearly passed on the healthier options. What exactly did they mean about second chances?

As I found a seat amongst soccer moms, giggling teens and a few loner business professionals, I ran a quick search on my phone. What was up with MOD? With 20-plus years of experience working with brands of all sizes and shapes, I was no stranger to clever branding, tasteful ambiance or friendly staff, but something seemed different here.

I didn't get far into my search before my pizza was ready. As I noshed, I resolved to get to the bottom of what was really happening at MOD — and a few weeks later, I finally found myself on the phone with co-founder Scott Svenson. As we chatted, that *second chances* line started to make sense.

While Scott and his wife Ally had owned successful restaurants in the past, they hadn't picked the idea of fast-dining artisanal pizza lightly. In fact, in 2008, Ally had even cautioned Scott that,

"the last thing the world needs is another soulless restaurant chain."

Scott shared the questions that formed the essence of MOD. What if everyone could get exactly what they wanted, made fresh on demand, for as little as possible? And what if employees were paid as much as possible and given real opportunities for growth, even second chances?

Second chances, there it was again, the subtle message I'd seen in the menu. Aside from guaranteeing you'd love your pizza or you could try again, MOD was hinting at the core of what their business believed. The deeper purpose at MOD wasn't to just make great pizza, but to put people first. MOD was all about being a "force for positive change in the lives and the communities we serve." But how exactly did they do this?

According to Scott, the positive change first started early on when his team was looking at what could be done about the high employee turnover rate standard to the food industry. Scott pointed out, "As any business owner knows, it's difficult to maintain a high standard of quality when employees leave as soon as they're trained."

As Scott and his team looked within their own ranks, they noticed a trend among some of their most committed employees; they might not have even been hired elsewhere. Due to their complicated histories, from resume gaps to brushes with the law, these people had found themselves struggling to find employment. At MOD, they received above-industry pay, benefits, and an empowering team environment. These employees were grateful and it showed in their work and how they treated guests. They were more patient, friendly and eager to serve. As Scott shared with me, "When we took care of our people, they took care of our customers." (We'll describe this shift and how they accomplished it in more detail in Section 7.)

After seeing this, Scott told his shareholders and advisors about the commitment to put people first. According to Scott, "This commitment was a little bit unconventional. There was definitely some risk and cost involved, but we believed over time we would get payback on those investments and build sustainable competitive advantage by virtue of making the purpose about the people."

The result of the people-first mission? By 2018, MOD had expanded rapidly to more than 404 stores across 28 states and the U.K., attained the title of fastest-growing pizza chain, and registered $398 million in system-wide sales, a 45 percent year-over-year increase. Plus, they earned a five-star review from this author.

By hiring those who might have otherwise been overlooked and paying them well, MOD created a sustainable business model while contributing to the community. MOD hit the sweet spot where purpose meets profit — where doing good is scalable and return on investment is no longer restricted to financial return.

MOD has zeroed in on an advantage not easily replicated by any other brand. That's not because of some closely held secret ingredient, but because MOD's very DNA is built on a strong purpose: a purpose that connects with their consumers, engages their employees, and drives innovation in the industry. MOD has achieved a Purpose Advantage™.

The Definition of Purpose

Before we go much further, let's get on the same page regarding purpose and how it works as a competitive advantage. According to *Webster's Dictionary*, purpose is defined as "an end to be attained," but there's more to it when it comes to brands.

First, purpose is *foundational*. It's not a gimmick — it's a clearly defined and long-term strategy that affects every part of the business, from innovation to product development to consumer experience to marketing. It connects with consumers' values and passions, attracting and retaining high-quality talent, spurring creativity, and driving growth. Purpose doesn't stop at the mission statement; it influences every decision at every level.

Second, purpose is an *action*, not a declaration. It requires brands to make meaningful change, not just launch a new ad campaign. While grammatically *purpose* is a noun, metaphorically, for the highest performing brands, it must be a verb.

Third, for purpose to create a real advantage, it must be *societal*. Societal is for the common good, in that it benefits society as a whole, not just for the good of certain individuals and sections of society. What do I mean by that?

There are plenty of brands out there with purpose-driven mission statements. For example, global makeup brand Glossier® is deeply rooted in its commitment to democratize beauty products for all. Its research and product development is centered around a commitment to listening to the desires of the consumer, not the board of directors. Instead of creating the skin creams and lip balms the company would like to sell, its researchers dig deep into what their consumers would like to purchase. A purpose like this, while profitable, is not inherently designed to promote societal good.

When we talk about purpose in this book, we're talking about the kind of purpose concerned with the well-being of others, the planet and our future. We mean missions for preserving the environment or fighting for social justice, the kind of purposes that make the world a better place.

While grammatically *purpose* is a noun, metaphorically, for the highest performing brands, it must be a verb.

One of the best examples of a purpose is Seventh Generation®.

Founded in 1988, Seventh Generation started with the goal of nurturing the health of the next seven generations and beyond. By creating natural, safe and organic cleaning products, Seventh Generation remains committed to providing clean without compromise. Through a combination of lobbying and product, logistical, and packaging innovation, Seventh Generation weaves the mission into every single thing they do.

I had the opportunity to sit down with CEO Joey Bergstein, who graciously shared his insight on what he refers to as a virtuous circle of mission (i.e. their purpose):

"Our mission drives our business and the business drives our mission. The truer we are to the mission, the better job we do at creating safe, effective and natural products. The better the products, both for the consumer and the environment, the better the business results, which we can then reinvest into innovating our products and the marketplace itself, bringing us back to our mission of nurturing the health of the next seven generations and beyond." SEE FIGURE 1

For Seventh Generation, purpose isn't something the company talks about, but something it does. It's a purpose foundational to every new initiative and benevolent to consumers, employees and the environment.

Purpose of nurturing the health of the next 7 generations and beyond

Create safe, natural, and effective products

Happy customers and happy earth

Better business results

Invest in innovation

FIGURE 1

Those intentional actions weren't just received with applause from consumers. They resulted in $250 million in annual sales, double-digit growth rates since 2006, and a $600 million acquisition by Unilever®.[1]

It's clear that a purpose like Seventh Generation's is working and consumers are ready to reward brands with similar qualities. But how did we reach a place where brands were taking part in conversations about the greater good?

It could be that competition has driven brands to new levels of emotional engagement. It could also be that organized religion has changed at a rate slower than consumer culture, leaving a purpose gap for millions of consumers who are now less engaged religiously. Regardless of how we got here, I do know, with certainty, that today's consumer is looking for more.

Since 2010, when I first led a research partnership between Barkley, Boston Consulting Group, and Service Management Group, I've been studying patterns in consumer behavior to see how Millennials and Generation Z have shifted the market in ways that influence all generations of buyers, including older consumers.

+ +
+   +
+   In all my research, "purpose" was and is a   +
+   recurring theme for consumers of all ages.   +
+   +
+ +

When I co-authored *Marketing to Millennials* in 2013, the landscape was completely different from how it was in 2018, when I published *Marketing to Gen Z*. Many brands that were winning in 2013 are nonexistent today. We are in an age where products and services are commodities as soon as they hit the market. Having the best product or the fastest service is no longer enough to make a brand strong. When consumers decide what to purchase, the values a brand stands for and the actions it takes to prove it will make that brand stand out.

In the next few pages, we will look at the role purpose plays for a values-driven consumer and how purpose often confers a sustainable advantage. Most importantly, we'll share the framework and exercises to help you adopt a Purpose Advantage for your own organization.

---

1   "Inside Seventh Generation's Quest to Blow Up Without Selling Out" Fortune, 2016, http://fortune.com/seventh-generation-green-cleaning-products/

THREE

The Modern Consumer

As consumers, we have a lot on our plates. From the moment we wake up, we're plagued with decisions, options and suggestions. There is effectively no limit to where advertisers can reach us, leaving us in a state of "shopping" nearly 24/7. Now that we can shout to Alexa to order wet wipes while elbow deep in a dirty diaper, or apply for a mortgage while waiting for an oil change, consumer expectations have evolved.

The modern shopping experience is more complicated than ever before. Just buying basic hygiene items brings with it such an incredible range of choices, all of which the modern consumer processes in seconds. Even buying a simple razor can lead to an internal dialogue that looks something like this...

What seems like a simple purchase can easily become a more complicated lifestyle decision. Even as consumers are comparing price, quality and features, at the same moment, they are considering brand, social proof and finally —the scariest of all — indirect competitors. Beard oil.

Many would blame the lack of brand loyalty (millennials and their lack of commitment have led to more brands and options, creating this current overwhelming state).

But given my research on the future of consumers, I can tell you with certainty that the "youths" aren't the ones to blame.

The blame really falls on all of us. We are emotional, illogical consumers. We'd all like to believe we're reasonable people who weigh all the options in order to make the most logical decisions. But alas, that is just not the case.

For example, on your grocery run, you decide you need some cereal. As you enter the breakfast foods aisle, you're quickly confronted with dozens and dozens of options. As you scan the shelves of brightly colored cereal boxes, if you were willing to do the math, you might first decide on an acceptable price per ounce. Then, in order to further sort your cereal options, you determine a flavor score for each brand in your set. Cereal Brand X tastes better than Cereal Brand Y, giving them scores of five and four, respectively. Within that flavor score, you award points based on the health of the option, or maybe penalize certain brands for sugar content. With the price per ounce, flavor score and some sense of health taken into account, you crunch the numbers on a spreadsheet and arrive at the perfect cereal option for you and your family.

Of course, it's likely you did none of those things. It's more likely you scanned the selection, recognized a brand, found the flavor you liked, and moved along.

Because after all, you're a modern consumer with places to be and bigger problems to solve. In most shopping situations, while we'd like to be analytical and make the most thorough decision, we just don't have the time. So we rely on our brains to think quickly and to take shortcuts in order to salvage any remaining brain power.

With modern consumers relying on fast thinking, many brands and companies have spent millions of dollars trying to become the instinctual and quick decision. But how does one infiltrate the fast thinking of the preoccupied consumer?

FOUR

The Modern Consumer Mindset

Recently, I had the opportunity to talk with the founders of Bombas® socks, Randy Goldberg and David Heath. Launched in 2013, Bombas is a sock manufacturer that follows the one-for-one model (more details on this model in Section 5), giving a pair of socks to the homeless for every pair purchased, and has seen incredible growth by getting to the heart of the modern consumer.

Because they made a better sock and added a dose of purpose, Bombas is now part of cultural conversations. At Barkley, we describe this fast-thinking decision process that goes into a purchase decision as the Modern Consumer Mindset. These six components (shown in **FIGURE 2**) help brands like Bombas visualize how consumers make decisions and where it's appropriate to influence purchasing decisions. Together, the six mindsets propel top performing brands.

Social Circle
Part of Cultural Conversation

Self
Emotional Connection

Innovative
The Useful New

Trusted
Puts Consumer Needs First

Accessible
Simplifies My Life

Purpose
Adding Good

FIGURE 2

The first component of the Modern Consumer Mindset is the consumer's **Social Circle**. This group of friends, family and other close-knit relations or acquaintances is one of the first considerations when interacting with a brand: "What will my friends think?" At Bombas, the design and features of the sock were manufactured in a way that would, according to Goldberg, "Change the way people talk about their socks."

As modern consumers shop, they are considering, at all times, what they've heard their friends discuss, both online and offline. When possible, consumers will pursue the brand or product that helps them fit more comfortably within their social circle. Social circle brands get a lot of word of mouth, and in today's age, word of mouse.

This recognition of how the modern consumer engages with their social circle gave Bombas the initial boost they needed with their first grassroots funding campaign on Indiegogo®, reaching $145,000 in support. The concept of the sock and the one-for-one model got people talking and engaging with each other about the brand.

While a little cheesy, word of mouse refers to how word of mouth has changed with the growth of social media.

Second, we have **Self**, the emotional connection consumers have with their identity and the way brands and products make them feel about themselves. "How will this brand make me feel?" Self is an important component as we talk about purpose, because in many ways, consumers feel better about themselves when the brands they support make positive choices on their behalf.

Bombas saw this clearly when launching the one-for-one model. For every pair of socks purchased, a pair is donated to a homeless shelter. Socks are one of the most in-demand items at homeless shelters, and due to hygiene restrictions, can't be a secondhand donation. This restriction means homeless shelters shell out a substantial chunk of their budget clothing the feet of the men, women and children.

However, in 2016, a donation center in North Carolina was able to save $10,000 and put two kids from the shelter system into college due to the savings from donated Bombas socks.

The modern consumer who buys from Bombas can feel a strong sense of self each time they don their brightly colored, quality socks.

Third, we consider **Innovation**. This component is where the consumer considers if the brand has continued to evolve and stay relevant in his or hers ever-changing life. The modern consumer is the master of reinvention, and expects their brand of choice to relate.

When it comes to innovation, Bombas truly excels. While the standard sock is crafted with low-quality materials, the guys behind Bombas pride themselves on their innovative designs and quality construction.

"Things like seamless toe, arch support, comfort foot pads, super high-quality fabrics, articulation of the heel — we hold all of these functions and features we found in really high end, sport-specific type of product and offer them to the general public," shared Heath. In addition to the great quality, Bombas boasts several engineered solutions for common sock problems such as the honeycomb arch support and blister tab, and the socks donated to the homeless have an anti-microbial treatment and reinforced seams.

Fourth is **Trust**. "Can I trust this brand will put my needs first?" As consumers become more aware and skeptical of brands, it's increasingly difficult to win and maintain trust. Millennials and Generation Z embrace tech and are now far more cautious when it comes to sharing their personal information.

Keeping trust alive is crucial for Bombas — once trust is lost, it is not easily regained. Bombas does a spectacular job of communicating its actions to consumers, as well as sharing donation numbers and actions clearly and consistently.

The fifth component is **Accessibility**. "Will this make my life easier?" When choosing between brands, the consumer not only looks at the product or service itself for ease of use, but the ease of the entire process. Is the brand easy to buy from? Will the brand be easy to engage with in the future? Will the technology integrate with existing products? At all touchpoints, the modern consumer expects the brand to remain easily accessible.

Again, Bombas and its smooth e-commerce platform shine when it comes to accessibility. Not only are the socks easy to purchase and use, the donated socks are delivered directly to the people who need them most.

Lastly, we have **Purpose**. This is the deeper meaning of the brand and one of the most important ways to connect with the modern consumer. Consumers ask themselves, "When I buy from this brand, what is the company doing on my behalf and what are they doing to better society?" At Bombas, the consumer understands immediately the deeper purpose of their purchase.

Millennials and Generation Z were the first to ask these hard questions of brand, and now we can expect all consumers to ask the same.

A common piece of fiction floating around about the modern consumer is the idea of infidelity: That somehow, without any real rhyme or reason, the modern consumer skips from brand to brand without a second thought. Traditional marketers can be heard crying, "They aren't brand loyal!"

In fact, the modern consumer is brand discerning—they continually evaluate all present options, regardless of how much they love their current brand.

The 29-year-old mom might love laundry detergent from Tide®, but that does not preclude her from exploring and testing the soapy waters of other brands promising better quality, price or purpose.

Just take a walk down the laundry aisle at Walmart® and you'll see the power of purpose at play. Seventh Generation and Tide, placed on the same shelf, technically offer the same product. According to reviews, both products offer a great clean and a suitable scent. In terms of branding, both products offer a strong and recognizable brand, especially Tide.

But when we crunch the numbers in FIGURE 3, we see Seventh Generation charges not quite a penny an ounce more. That's just under a 10 percent premium. And for what?

For that extra penny, Seventh Generation offers a meaningful and relevant purpose, to boot. Flip the white bottle around and you'll see a label designed to demonstrate, not "advertise" their purpose. All ingredients are listed in clear and easy-to-understand language. Even the color of the bottle itself speaks to the purpose. Seventh Generation is doing things differently to create a cleaner, safer world.

Despite the Tide brand controlling almost a fifth of total U.S. liquid laundry detergent sales in 2018, Seventh Generation is able to charge a premium for a comparable product, simply because of its commitment to safe and clean products that prevent harm to the planet.[2]

Seventh Generation isn't the first to see this kind of advantage. A recent study by Unilever looked at 20,000 people around the world and found the majority of people genuinely care about sustainability. "Over half of all consumers already buy or want to buy sustainably, 33 percent already purchase products with sustainability in mind and a further 21 percent do not currently, but would like to."[3]

$13.94
at Walmart
(115 fl oz)

$12.99
at Walmart
(100 fl oz)

FIGURE 3

According to the 2018 Purpose Premium Index by Porter Novelli/Cone, Americans not only think highly of purpose-driven companies, but are "willing to reward them in a number of ways."[4]

And if you're wondering if it's just the young people calling for purpose, analysts at Forrester® can put your mind to rest with recent research showing older generations are growing more sensitive to company values, with four in 10 Younger Boomers considering company purpose before making a purchase. **FIGURE 4**

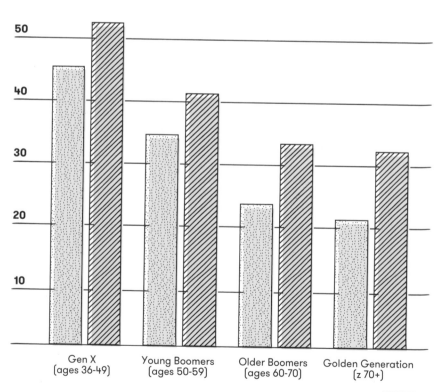

FIGURE 4

It's important to note here that purpose alone is not enough. Purpose is only a valid differentiator when all else is equal. Brands who live their purpose well understand a Purpose Advantage is simultaneously functional (meets their needs as a consumer), emotional (evokes an emotional response), and societal (contains a deeper purpose).

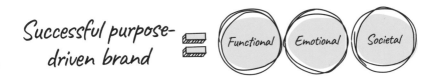

Successful purpose-driven brand = Functional Emotional Societal

Only when all three elements are present does the Purpose Advantage truly begin to play out.

---

2 "Sales share of the leading 10 liquid laundry detergent brands of the United States in 2018" Statista.com, 2018, https://www.statista.com/statistics/251472/sales-share-of-the-leading-10-liquid-laundry-detergent-brands-of-the-us/

3 "Making Purpose Pay: Inspiring Sustainable Living" Unilever.com, 2018, https://www.unilever.com/Images/making-purpose-pay-inspiring-sustainable-living-170515_tcm244-506419_en.pdf

4 "Porter Novelli/Cone Purpose Premium Index" Cone Communications, 13 November 2018, http://www.conecomm.com/research-blog/purpose-premium

FIVE

Purpose and the Modern Consumer

Purpose isn't new. We've seen brands engaging in these conversations more and more in the past 10 years. Non-profits, Certified B Corporations, corporate social responsibility initiatives, and cause marketing have become commonplace.

FIVE

"Doing good" is no longer reserved for non-profits, but is now expected of influential brands trying to build emotional connections.

Larry Fink, founder, chairman and CEO of BlackRock, Inc.®, said this in his 2019 letter to CEOs:

"Profits are in no way inconsistent with purpose - in fact, profits and purpose are inextricably linked. Profits are essential if a company is to effectively serve all of its stakeholders over time - not only shareholders, but also employees, customers, and communities.

"Similarly, when a company truly understands and expresses its purpose, it functions with the focus and strategic discipline that drive long term profitability. Purpose unifies management, employees, and communities. It drives ethical behavior and creates an essential check on actions that go against the best interests of stakeholders. Purpose guides culture, provides a framework for consistent decision-making, and, ultimately, helps sustain long-term financial returns for the shareholders of your company."[5]

B Corporation certification (also known as B Lab certification or B Corp certification) is a private certification issued to for-profit companies by B Lab, a global nonprofit organization. The B Lab certification requires companies to meet social sustainability and environmental performance standards, meet accountability standards, and to be transparent to the public according to the score they receive on the assessment.

We tend to use the word consumer, but left the word "customer" due to the fact that it is a quote.

For the CEO of a major investment firm to describe corporate purpose as inextricably linked with profits means we're looking at a radical shift — not only in the way businesses craft their mission statements, but how they manage suppliers, package products, relate to communities, and build their brands.

To further reinforce this shift, a recent study conducted by Cone Communications stated that more than 60 percent of consumers not only want, but expect corporations and brands to take the lead in tackling social and environmental change.[6] And 76 percent of those surveyed said they would "decline to do business with a company if it held views and supported issues that conflicted with their beliefs."

Purpose is here, and we can't avoid it.

But adopting purpose means more than just paying lip service to pro-social initiatives. And that's where the problem lies.

In the past few years, we've seen brands attempt to jump into controversial, purpose-based conversations via cause marketing. While some brands walk away net-positive, having won over new consumers and loyal followers, others have left the scene visibly damaged.

At face value, cause marketing seems like an easy win for most brands. Find a cause or conversation worth joining, contribute in some capacity, create advertisements highlighting your involvement, and reap the positive rewards, both financial and altruistic. For example, think of Dove's *Campaign for Real Beauty®* and Yoplait's *Save Lids to Save Lives®*.

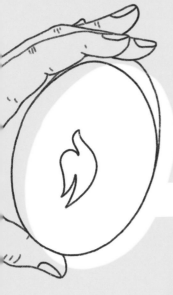

Real Beauty™

DOVE'S CAMPAIGN FOR REAL BEAUTY

Dove® launched the Campaign for Real Beauty in 2004, in response to the findings of a major global study, "The Real Truth About Beauty: A Global Report," which had revealed that only two percent of women around the world would described themselves as beautiful. The main message of the Dove campaign was that women's unique differences should be celebrated, rather than ignored, and that physical appearance should be transformed from a source of anxiety to a source of confidence. This message was delivered through a variety of mediums, including TV commercials, magazine spreads, talk shows, and a worldwide conversation via the internet.

YOPLAIT'S SAVE LIDS TO SAVE LIVES

General Mills®, Yoplait's parent company, contributed over $50 million over 15 years through its sponsorship of Susan G. Komen's Race for the Cure® series and by donating 10 cents to breast cancer efforts each time a consumer sent in a special pink lid from one of its yogurt cups. This program was phased out.

Save Lids to Save Lives™

Both are examples of mature brands leveraging their position in an industry to make positive change. For Dove, the end goal was to challenge societal standards of beauty. For Yoplait®, the end goal was to combat cancer.

While it would be nice to say these brands were partaking in these campaigns for pure altruistic reasons, as with any cause marketing campaign, their core motivation was sales growth. For Dove, the Campaign for Real Beauty evolved and over time has had lasting impact on what the brand stands for, how it develops and markets its products.[7]

For many brands, cause marketing can be hugely helpful in terms of gaining credibility, authority and loyalty. Brands doing a positive thing or taking meaningful action, when executed correctly, can turn the hearts, eyes, ears and wallets of consumers in their favor.

However, when the cause isn't properly marketed, we find many brands dealing with a case of the "leaky bucket."

For example, many brands donate a portion of their proceeds to charity. It's not uncommon to read a press release detailing how Brand X donated 1 percent of proceeds to Charity Y. These initiatives can have a positive impact on the cause, but often lack a deep connection with the brand itself, making it easy for the consumer to forget who donated the money, who was responsible, and why the company was involved in the cause in the first place. Their credit for the positive action leaks.

I've seen the leaky bucket at work in my own life. As a long-time client of American Century® Investments, I was flabbergasted to discover how much good the investment firm was doing on my behalf. Aside from providing me with investment services, American Century was donating 40 percent of company profit to medical research. A whopping 40 percent! Not many brands can boast those kinds of numbers, yet there I was, absolutely clueless to the good my investment manager was doing. In fact, since its birth, American Century has donated over $1.5 billion to the Stowers Institute for Medical Research®, a world-class cancer research organization.

In the case of American Century, while the cause is being achieved, the campaign is missing the second half of the strategy. American Century is failing to use the positive energy from its pro-social efforts to drive more business. If I had known my investment company was so actively pursuing a cure for cancer, I would have felt a deeper connection with their mission, and thus, felt comfortable — if not proud — giving them a greater share of my wallet.

These credit leaks, depending on their severity, ultimately hurt the brand's ability to continue to participate in the cause it originally pursued.

Even more common than failing to market one's efforts, like American Century, is the problem of overmarketing and underdelivering. If failing to market properly is the leaky bucket, then over-marketing is a bottomless bucket. It's the company pouring resources into a campaign designed to generate positive brand energy while doing none of the actual work required to make a difference.

Let's bring in a favorite brand to talk about the bottomless bucket. In its campaign, "Race Together," Starbucks® made a classic cause marketing error, the most common mistake we see with larger brands eager to show results quickly.

Starbucks took credit for action they hadn't yet taken.

We see this often with brands looking to jump into a conversation they aren't yet ready to lead. By pushing the marketing portion saying, "Hey, we're doing a nice thing!" before having actually done the nice thing, many brands not only miss out on fueling brand energy but face an enraged backlash. In these cases, no amount of press releases, strategic advertising or Twitter® apologies can fill the bottomless bucket.

STARBUCKS, RACE TOGETHER CAMPAIGN

The Race Together campaign aimed to spark a national conversation about race relations by having baristas write the phrase "Race Together" on Starbucks cups. The company also published "Conversation Starters" in USA Today. However, at the time of the campaign kick-off, Starbucks had done very little in terms of reconciling racial tensions in their own company and was thus subject to a great deal of backlash.

#RaceTogether

Both the leaky and bottomless bucket are not a result of a faulty purpose or a company with ill-will. They happen when a company has a purpose but no strategy. And when we talk purpose with strategy, no discussion would be complete with discussing TOMS® shoes.

---

5   Fink, Larry, "Purpose & Profit" Letter to CEOs, 17 January 2019, https://www.blackrock.com/corporate/investor-relations/larry-fink-ceo-letter

6   "2017 Cone Communications CSR Study" Cone, 17 May 2017, http://www.conecomm.com/2017-cone-communications-csr-study-pdf

7   Announcing the Dove Real Beauty Pledge. (17, June 13). Retrieved June 17, 19, from https://www.unilever.com/news/news-and-features/Feature-article/2017/Announcing-the-Dove-Real-Beauty-Pledge.html

TOMS SHOES

Founded in 2006, the company designs and sells shoes (based on the Argentine alpargata design), eyewear, coffee, apparel and handbags. When TOMS sells a pair of shoes, a new pair of shoes is given to an impoverished child. When TOMS sells eyewear, part of the profit is used to save or restore eyesight for people in developing countries.

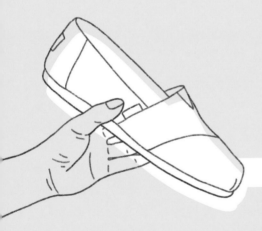

One for One™

SIX

The BOGO Trap

TOMS was the first mover in the one-for-one, or buy-one-give-one (BOGO), purpose-driven brand evolution. The BOGO model is simple; for every item that a consumer purchases, the company donates a comparable item to a group or individual in need. With the BOGO model, the small premium of the product's pricing is quickly outweighed in the consumer's mind as a reasonable cost to serve their own needs even as they provide for a less fortunate individual. Instead of writing a check to the impoverished, the consumer pays TOMS, expecting TOMS to help the unfortunate on their behalf.

The model works because as the purpose is achieved, profits increase for the brand. As profits increase, more social good is achieved.

However, the BOGO model can quickly become a trap for many brands. The model seduces many brands with promises of big returns and big impact, yet leaves too many with serious financial woes and devastating public relations missteps.

In many cases, as consumers buy more items, the "giving" portion becomes increasingly expensive to execute due to the scaling of distribution costs. At that point, brands either watch their margins wither away or pass the additional premium on to the consumer — a consumer who was already paying a premium.

While we can say with confidence that TOMS found success with the BOGO model, the one-for-one model is just one way to approach integrating purpose and not the gold standard. Because, in addition to financial obstacles, the BOGO model also fails to take into consideration the true costs associated with giving.

It may sound crazy at first, but every action a brand takes, even a positive social-good action, can have negative consequences. In the case of TOMS, giving impoverished children free footwear sounded like a no-brainer. The shoes could prevent the spread of disease, help children travel to education, and so on. But TOMS failed to see the economic impact of injecting free goods into an already unstable economy. By giving shoes, it caused local shoemakers to instantly see demand collapse, hurting their ability to function as a business.[8] So while TOMS was helping, they were also hurting. As a response, TOMS has begun its expand to eyewear, in hopes of combatting the negative outcomes of their shoe donations.

The BOGO method, while it can be effective, it is often short-sighted and lacks a holistic approach to doing the most good as a brand.

---

8   Reed, Russel, "One -for-Non: Aid Dependency and the 'TOMS Model'", Harvard Political Review, 22 March 2017, http://harvardpolitics.com/world/one-for-none/

SEVEN

The Purpose
Advantage™

It's clear existing methods of incorporating purpose are insufficient, risky, and in some cases, borderline ineffective, not because these companies' leaders don't care, but simply because cause marketing and corporate social responsibility as we know them are not good enough.

While a few marketing principles still reign true today — the classic four Ps aren't going anywhere — we propose embedding a P necessary to appeal to the modern consumer. Purpose.

In today's transparent, digital world, purpose = words + action. It's not just what you say, but how you prove it through what you do. Purpose goes beyond communication to guide business behavior and company culture to deliver better business performance.

Brands, both young and mature, have the opportunity to weave purpose deep into their DNA, leading to powerful profits and deeper connections with consumers. Existing strategies fall short because they fail to connect the purpose to every part of the business.

In the last ten years, the pattern has gone like this:

one	New brands and startups "bake" the purpose into their business model, often following a one-for-one approach. These new brands then struggle to juggle the economies of scale and never really break into mature brand status, putting a cap on their ability to "do good."
two	Mature brands, recognizing the need to give back, and to participate in larger conversations, sometimes delegate the "purpose stuff" to their marketing team. They offer up some arbitrary percentage of earnings and offload a similar amount to promote their positive actions. Some smarter and mature brands take the route of corporate social responsibility initiatives, but at the end of the day, most mature brands still end up with corporate social good siloed off from their brand purpose.

Purpose is taken care of in "that" department, leaving a small group of leaders rolling the dice in terms of how the general public will respond. When it comes time to measure the success of the campaign, leaders may fail to see a return on the investment and either hit "delete" on the program or allocate it to a smaller department.

With both of these approaches, whether in a big company or a small one, the potential to do the most good is limited, both socially and financially. The solution isn't to develop a new program or initiative, but to integrate purpose right into the brand itself. This is the Purpose Advantage™.

A clearly defined Purpose Advantage is foundational to connecting with consumers' values and passions. When well executed, a Purpose Advantage is key to attracting and retaining high-quality talent, spurring creativity, and driving growth.

If you're rolling your eyes at the idea of one strategy accomplishing so many things, keep this in mind: this is not a new fad, trend, or clever way of organizing your business. It's not a gimmick or something to hand off to your human resource department.

A Purpose Advantage is a clearly defined and long-term strategy that affects every part of the business, from innovation to product development to consumer experience to marketing.

And with that, there must be alignment around purpose across all departments and business lines. Everyone within a company, including leadership, is responsible for bringing purpose to life.

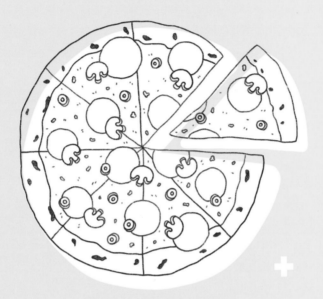

Let's go full circle and look closer at the case of MOD from Section One. At MOD, there were issues early on with the purpose living itself out.

As is the case with most fast-casual restaurants, it was increasingly difficult for MOD to retain quality team members. This revolving door of associates left their consumers with poor experiences, their teams short staffed, and their people-first mission suffering.

While leadership was on board with the people-first mission, it's clear the company wasn't living out the purpose at all levels. So instead of management throwing up their hands and giving up, they used the problem as an opportunity to further their mission and purpose: to put people first. And in this situation, given that they were dealing specifically with people problems, the natural next step became asking the hard questions.

Why are our employees leaving? What makes employees stick around? What makes them love spreading their MODness?

In many instances, fast food employment served as a transitionary type of employment: employees were leaving for better pay. Even if they liked MOD, they saw better opportunities elsewhere.

So MOD's executives talked to an employee who had stuck around the longest, and what they found surprised them. This devoted, consistent and joyful employee was grateful for his job at MOD in a way most other employees weren't. This particular employee had a history of difficulty with the law, and thus, struggled to find employment, especially employment that offered a livable wage. In many ways, MOD had offered dignity and opportunities typically reserved only for those with a clean record. By hiring someone who needed a second chance, MOD discovered the solution to its tension point, solved a turnover issue, and continued its mission of serving people first.

This "second chance" philosophy not only expanded the hiring pool to those with special needs, but created a workforce of employees genuinely excited to be there. And by taking it a step further and investing in its employees, MOD found itself with some of the lowest turnover rates in its industry sector. MOD founder Scott shared the company's approach to hiring:

"We believe we are just in the very early innings of what we can do with turnover over time, first and foremost with our general managers, then secondly with our captains, and then with our squad. There is always going to be a natural level of turnover. And what we're trying to distinguish is negative turnover — we've lost somebody who we wanted to stay with us — versus positive turnover, which is somebody who's using MOD as a bridge to some place they want to be.

"They come in because maybe they were homeless. Or maybe they were transitioning out of rehab. Or maybe they were transitioning out of a bad relationship. And they come to MOD, and they use MOD as a stabilizing force, where they get back on their feet, and they build their confidence, and they build some resources. And then six, twelve, eighteen months later, they move onto something even better. That's turnover we celebrate because when it comes back to the mission of what we're trying to do, we're not trying to in an unnatural way hold onto our people.

"If there is an opportunity for them to springboard to something even better in their life, we want MOD to be that bridge that helps them get there. And so we try to be thoughtful about how we think about turnover, and minimize or reduce negative turnover — and celebrate positive turnover."

By acknowledging and addressing its flaws, MOD was able to not only solve a problem, but identify an advantage largely unknown to the industry thus far.

✣✣✣✣✣✣✣✣✣✣✣✣✣✣✣✣✣✣✣✣✣✣✣✣✣✣✣✣✣✣✣✣✣✣✣
✣ **Its purpose became its advantage.** ✣
✣✣✣✣✣✣✣✣✣✣✣✣✣✣✣✣✣✣✣✣✣✣✣✣✣✣✣✣✣✣✣✣✣✣✣

Unfortunately, the process of implementing a Purpose Advantage is not a one-size-fits-all formula. We can't hit copy and paste on what MOD did and hope to see success with every company and every brand. The Purpose Advantage is not a simple "do this, get that," strategy. In fact, it's more of a journey of self-discovery, both for the leaders and the employees, and in some cases, for the consumers.

The general approach goes like this:

---

one | Get to know your consumer on a deep level. Get clear on what they want—including all need states—today and tomorrow.

---

two | Frame the meaning of purpose for your organization. First, look at what society at large views as a worthy purpose, then look inward at your company's past, and then ask your consumers what really matters to them.

---

three | Compose a Purpose Statement. It doesn't have to be long or complicated, but craft a meaningful statement to explain your why more clearly.

---

four | Pressure test the purpose. Every brand will implement this differently, but the main goal is the same. Take your purpose and apply it to every department, function, team, process and initiative. How does your purpose impact existing procedures? What changes need to take place in order to live the purpose out fully?

---

five | Lean in. Create metrics and rewards that support the new purpose and get leadership on board.

If this sounds oversimplified, it's because it absolutely is an attempt to boil it down.

Five steps does not do the process justice. I've spent hours and hours with brands, getting clear on their consumers and why they exist. It's not simple or easy, but it's incredibly powerful.

I wouldn't call it an advantage if it was easy, would I?

With that being the case, more theories and abstract examples won't help you get clear on your Purpose Advantage. Doing the work will. In an ideal world, I could sit down with each and every one of you and discuss where you've been, where you're going, and how to strategically implement a Purpose Advantage.

But alas, teleportation is still a few years away. So in lieu of a face-to-face meeting, I offer you the complete framework, materials, and activities — known as the Purpose Advantage Workshop™ — to use as you see fit. This workshop is packed with examples, practical steps and even more guidance on how to ensure your Purpose Advantage is executed to perfection.

EIGHT

The Purpose Advantage™ Workshop

Building your Purpose Advantage, in its purest form, is the action you take to live out your brand purpose. In its more detailed form (as it works in real life), your Purpose Advantage is a complex, nuanced and people-driven set of activities. Its end goal is enabling permanent and strategic change in how your company and employees behave.

In a recent partnership with the Association of National Advertisers (ANA) Center for Brand Purpose, we created a workshop designed to help marketers with the complex task of identifying and instituting a brand purpose beyond profits.

I present the four key frameworks and several exercises from that workshop here. This is, in many ways, a distillation of our best methods to engage people within an organization to create an authentic and effective Purpose Advantage. Intended to span one full day, this workshop is rooted in the research and knowledge we've acquired through our past experience.

My hope is that you find these ideas and exercises useful, and that you may adopt some as you work on a Purpose Advantage for your own organization.

The sample workshop uses key frameworks for exploring your impact, brand origin and consumer. These exercises will help you build a brief and discover your brand purpose. Teams will also collaborate and ideate on the creation of a Proof Plan™ that will bring it to life inside and outside their organizations.

The agenda is arranged as follows:

FRAMEWORK 1
World View — Setting Your Compass

FRAMEWORK 2
Identifying Your Brand Origin

FRAMEWORK 3
Evaluating Your Consumer Need

FRAMEWORK 4
Brand Archetype

PURPOSE STATEMENT EXERCISE

PROOF PLAN™ INSIDE EXERCISE

PROOF PLAN™ OUTSIDE EXERCISE

PROOF PLAN™ MEASURE EXERCISE

THE PITCH EXERCISE

While this workshop was designed to work with brand marketers and strategy leaders, you can expand elements of it to include anyone looking to better understand how to create a brand purpose and enhance or develop unifying internal strategies and external communications. In fact, it's best if you assemble a cross-functional team from throughout your organization to engage in the process. In order for purpose to permeate your organization, guide behavior and impact business, collaboration from across the company is imperative.

Each framework is broken into three sections:

one	An essential question your teams should feel comfortable answering post-learning.
two	Presentation of material or information specific to your organization for participants to consider.
three	A guided activity that will naturally spur discussion.

If you're planning to use this within your own organization, I recommend grounding participants in the Modern Consumer Mindset and Purpose Advantage, with examples shared within this text. An ice breaker, like writing personal purpose statements, is also effective in getting participants in the proper mindset before you begin your collaboration on the frameworks.

FRAMEWORK 1

World View – Setting Your Compass

GUIDING QUESTION

What is the potential of your product/service to solve a societal need?

"We've long held data that shows if you invest in purpose, you're able to attract better talent, retain the people you have, and drive sales. This is what millennials expect."

Emily Callahan
Chief Marketing & Experience Officer at St. Jude's Children Research Hospital®

Unlocking the power of purpose begins with understanding your business's value chain and its impact on global issues. In this framework, your team's familiarity with these two concepts is important to get the most out of the work.

While some of your team members may have a more holistic view, others may only be engaged in a portion of the value chain – that is, all the activities a business engages in to deliver its product or service; from sourcing raw materials through production, consumer use and disposal. It was introduced by Michael Porter in the 1970s as a tool to define competitive advantage. Today, it can be used to unlock the power of purpose by understanding the value chain of your business and how people and the planet are affected, and profit is created across your activities and business functions.

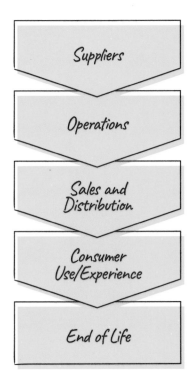

FIGURE 5

The second concept for this framework relates to global issues. In 2015, the General Assembly of the U.N. adopted the 2030 Agenda for Sustainable Development and outlined 17 **Sustainable Development Goals (SDGs)**.[10] These goals were created to unite business, governments and organizations on the most pressing issues of our time.

The idea is that by providing common language and targets, the global community can be united in action to drive better outcomes. When companies focus on a purpose that is rooted in creating value for others, improving the world we live in and inspiring the organization at all levels, they may increase their ability to drive profits and create sustainable value.

While these goals were designed for the U.N. and its functions, the outlined goals offer brands and businesses a clear list of where help is needed globally and locally, and what goals are worth pursuing.

The goals listed are:

1. No Poverty
2. Zero Hunger
3. Good Health & Well-being
4. Quality Education
5. Gender Equality
6. Clean Water & Sanitation
7. Affordable & Clean Energy
8. Decent Work & Economic Growth
9. Industry, Innovation & Infrastructure

10. Reduced Inequalities
11. Sustainable Cities & Communities
12. Responsible Consumption
   & Production
13. Climate Action
14. Life Below Water
15. Life on Land
16. Peace, Justice & Strong Institutions
17. Partnerships for the Goals

In this module, you can either present the United Nations Sustainable Development Goals via a workshop or print out the cards by visiting www.un.org/sustainabledevelopment/news/communications-material/.

FIGURE 6

ACTIVITY

one   Think about your organization's value chain. What are the core activities that make up your business? Make any changes to **FIGURE 7** to fit your business.

two   Using the impact boxes in **FIGURE 7**, note how your brand impacts people, the planet and profit along your value chain.

three	Now using the Sustainable Development Goals, select the most relevant SDGs to your value chain.

four

Business Functions:
Governance (senior Leadership), HR, Procurement, Research & Development

		Suppliers:	Operations:	Sales & Distribution:	Consumer Use/Experience:	End of Life:
	Core Activities					
	Impact					
	SDGs					

FIGURE 7

✛ Use this chart to create a framework that fits the needs of your situation.

DISCUSSION QUESTIONS

one   What are potential impacts in the sourcing of raw materials/
manufacturing/product use for your product or service?

two   What insights and information do you have today about
these impacts?

three   What information do you think you would want to know
about these impacts?

_____

_____

_____

_____

_____

four   What is the potential for your product/service to solve a
world/societal challenge?

_____

_____

_____

_____

five   What would you change about how you operate today?

FRAMEWORK 2

Identifying Your Brand Origin

GUIDING QUESTION

How does revisiting your brand origin story and previous actions inspire your purpose today?

"Understand and appreciate your brand's heritage and DNA. Define your brand purpose and the role you want to play in consumers' lives."

Lili Tomovich

Chief Experience Officer at MGM Resorts Worldwide®

Purpose is not the sole territory of new small businesses; mature businesses can establish credibility by rooting their purpose in an authentic company history. Is there a founder of the company? What were their original intentions in setting up the company? How has the company evolved over time? Your purpose can be forged by connecting or reconnecting with that original intention.

Unilever recently went through the process of finding its purpose and began by looking at where they started. According to Philippa Marshall, former Sustainability Business Director at Unilever, "By looking back, Unilever was able to see their role in the future."

For Unilever, their origin story went back all the way to 1885, when their British founder, William Lever, launched the first branded soap, Sunlight. Sunlight leveraged a patented technology to provide vegetable based soap at an affordable price. The product democratized basic hygiene, and led Lever to pursue the deeper purpose *of making cleanliness commonplace.*[11]

By understanding why Unilever began, leaders in the 21st century were able to craft a meaningful and relevant purpose of, "Making sustainable living commonplace." Learn more at *unilever.com/about/who-we-are/our-history/*

For this workshop, consider using the Unilever example as a jumping off point, or consider doing some work ahead of time to find out about your company founder's origins and examples of activity in social and environment impact you are already engaged in. Present what you learned with the group.

DISCUSSION QUESTIONS

Answer the following questions as a group:

one   How did your brand get its start?

two   Who were the people the brand was created to serve?

three   What did the product/service enable people to do?

_____

_____

_____

_____

_____

four   In addition to the product/service, what activities supported
         fulfillment of the need then, and are there SDGs relevant to
         the origin?

_____

_____

_____

_____

_____

FRAMEWORK 3
Evaluating Your Consumer Need

GUIDING QUESTION

What are the consumer interests and human needs your product/service fulfills in people's lives?

"Purpose is not empty words on a poster or lots of beautiful poetry. It's the filter for every action a company takes. No company in the world can navigate 360 degrees of conflict at the speed of technology without a clearly defined purpose."

Antonio Lucio
Former global CMO at HP and current global CMO at Facebook®

The modern consumer is presented with a bewildering amount of choices in today's marketplace. To ensure our products meet the needs of today's value-based consumer, we need to understand what it is they value. The business you are in is defined by what the consumer wants, not what you're selling. What we desire is a clean house, not a cleaning product. Ultimately, your future competitor might not be another product, but a cleaning service, or even a self-cleaning house.

To define purpose, we need to go beyond function, to think about the problem we're solving for people as they go about their daily lives. What choices would they make if we didn't exist?

For this framework, I suggest doing the pre-work beforehand to learn more about your core target consumer—the people your brand serves today and the functional and emotional benefits your product/service provides. Share these findings with your team during the workshop to aid them during the activity.

ACTIVITY

Explore your consumer even further with these fill-in-the-blank statements:

one   My consumer's values are _____,

_____ and _____.

two   My consumer would like to see _____

_____

_____ change in the world during their lifetime.

three   My consumer likes to help others by

_____

_____

_____.

DISCUSSION QUESTIONS

one   What values are most important to my consumer?

two   What changes do they want to see in the world?

three Where do they see opportunities to help others?

_____

_____

_____

_____

_____

four What actions do they take to make the world a better place?

_____

_____

_____

_____

_____

five   Write the higher purpose goal of your product/service
             through the eyes of a consumer.

_____

_____

_____

_____

_____

six   What are the most relevant SDGs for your consumer?

_____

_____

_____

_____

_____

FRAMEWORK 4

Brand Archetype

GUIDING QUESTION

How does who you are today dictate how you should frame the way you communicate and live your purpose?

"Nothing inspires people more than purpose and meaning. As a brand, if you can emulate a human and bring out your meaning — your corporate soul — it resonates."

Alicia Hatch
CMO at Deloitte Digital®

Storytelling is core to who we are as humans. It's how we learn and make sense of the world around us. Archetypes are characters from stories, evolved over millennia, that we emotionally respond to and recognize intuitively. By applying archetypes in this module, we can set the right tone for engagement on purpose and set the stage for the right intention on action.

We've categorized the archetypes of over 50 brands in order to show how understanding your brand's archetype can help you define the role you can play on issues/values that are important to you, your consumers, and society. Understanding this can shape the intent of your purpose and the actions you take to support it.

The following 12 purpose-driven brand archetypes used in the exercises in this framework are based on Carl Jung, but refined through the eyes of brand strategists behind the book, *The Hero and the Outlaw*, as well as the book *Archetypes in Branding*.[12, 13]

For this workshop, spend time discussing the brands and their corresponding archetypes before diving into the activity.

CAREGIVER

Characterized by the unselfish concern and/or devotion to nurture and care for others.

---

archetype family:

Angel, Guardian, Healer, Samaritan

---

keywords:

Altruism, compassion, patience, empathy, self-care, self-acceptance, generosity, connection

---

examples:

Johnson & Johnson® exists to spark solutions that create a better, healthier world.
Seventh Generation exists to nurture the health of the next seven generations.
Southwest Airlines® exists to connect people to what's important in their lives®.

CITIZEN

Driven by a deeply instilled sense of
personal integrity, fairness, equity
and responsibility to the community.

---

archetype
family:
Advocate, Everyman, Networker, Servant

---

keywords:
Stewardship, respect, fairness, accountability, conscious
change agent

---

examples:
TOMS exists to address the needs of children
and their communities around the world.
Whole Foods® exists to nourish people and the planet.
Salesforce® exists to drive equality for all.

CREATOR

Possesses a passionate need for self-expression, to be a cultural pioneer.

---

archetype
family:

Artist, Entrepreneur, Storyteller, Visionary

---

keywords:

Creativity, imagination, nonconformity, distinct aesthetic

---

examples:

LEGO® exists to inspire and develop
the builders of tomorrow.
HP® exists to engineer experiences that amaze.
IKEA® exists to democratize design.

INNOCENT

Pure, virtuous and faultless, free from
the responsibility of having done anything
hurtful or wrong.

---

archetype
family:

Child, Dreamer, Idealist, Muse

---

keywords:

Unbridled sense of wonder, purity, trust,
honesty, wholesomeness

---

examples:

Method exists to create happy, healthy homes.
Evian® exists to rejuvenate people and the planet, today,
tomorrow and always.

EXPLORER

Motivated by a powerful craving for
new experiences.

---

archetype
family:

Adventurer, Generalist, Pioneer, Seeker

---

keywords:

Independence, bravery, no limits, individualistic,
innovation, freedom

---

examples:

REI® exists to inspire, educate and outfit for a lifetime of
outdoor adventure and stewardship.
Clif Bar® exists to create a healthier, more sustainable world.
Starbucks exists to inspire and nurture the human spirit.

HERO

Acts to redeem society by overcoming great odds by completing acts of strength, courage and goodness.

---

archetype family:	Athlete, Liberator, Rescuer, Warrior

---

keywords:	Self-sacrifice, courage, transformation, strength, stamina

---

examples:	Nike® exists to bring inspiration and innovation to every athlete in the world. PayPal® exists to empower people and businesses to join and thrive in the global economy. Patagonia® exists to save our home planet.

JESTER

Seeks to lighten up the world by joyfully living in the moment.

---

archetype family:

Clown, Entertainer, Provocateur, Shapeshifter

---

keywords:

Wicked humor, irreverence, boldly original

---

examples:

Ben & Jerry's® exists to initiate innovative ways to improve the quality of life locally, nationally and internationally. THINX® exists to empower every body.

LOVER

Possesses an unbridled appreciation and affection for beauty, closeness and collaboration.

---

archetype family: | Companion, Hedonist, Matchmaker, Romantic

---

keywords: | Faithfulness, passionate, sexual, spiritual, vitality, appreciation

---

examples: | Haagen-Dazs® exists to transform the finest ingredients into extraordinary experiences.
Subaru® exists to show love and respect to all people.
Dove exists make beauty a source of our confidence, not anxiety.

MAGICIAN

Driven to understand the fundamental laws of the universe in order to make dreams into a reality.

---

archetype family:

Alchemist, Engineer, Innovator, Scientist

---

keywords:

Charisma, awe-inspiring intuition and cleverness, objective, ability to dream enormous dreams, beyond ordinary

---

examples:

MAC® Cosmetics exists to celebrate diversity and individuality.
Google® exists to make the world's information universally accessible and useful.
Disney® exists to create happiness for others.

REBEL

A force to be reckoned with, representing a voice that's had enough.

---

archetype
family:

Activist, Gambler, Maverick, Reformer

---

keywords:

Leadership, risk taking, candid, experimental, progressive and provocative, bravery

---

examples:

Levi's® exists to build a culture just as inspiring as the people who wear our jeans.
Virgin® exists to change business for good.
Harley Davidson® exists to fulfill dreams of personal freedom.

SAGE

Gently shares great wisdom with compassion to illuminate a path where mistakes are not repeated.

---

archetype family:

Detective, Mentor, Shaman, Translator

---

keywords:

Wisdom, intelligence, truth seeking, rational, researcher, prudence

---

examples:

National Geographic® exists to provide for humanity and the untold millions of other species with which we live.
TED® exists to make great ideas accessible and spark conversation.
BBC® exists to help people understand and engage with the world around them.

SOVEREIGN

A model of proper behavior while exuding an untouchable quality of privilege and royalty.

archetype family:	Ambassador, Judge, Patriarch, Ruler

keywords:	Rank, tradition, benevolence, nobility, inherited responsibility, stability

examples:	Volvo® exists to protect people. Brooks Brothers® exists to enhance the lives both within and beyond the communities we serve. Microsoft® exists to empower every person and every organization on the planet to achieve more.

All twelve illustrations were inspired by *The Hero and the Outlaw* and *Archetypes in Branding,* created by the Barkley Design & Experience team.[12, 13]

ACTIVITY

Decide which archetype best suits your brand.

DISCUSSION QUESTIONS

What implications does your archetype have on:

---

one   How you approach/tackle issues you impact?

---

two   Your brand voice and language?

_____

_____

_____

_____

_____

three   How you engage with your consumer?

_____

_____

_____

_____

_____

PURPOSE STATEMENT EXERCISE

GUIDING QUESTION

What is your Purpose Statement?

"People expect brands to do good for society and for the planet. Brands really have the opportunity and responsibility to step up and do so in a way that's good for growth."

Marc Pritchard
Chief Brand Officer at P&G®

So far, we've explored the impact we have on the world (world view), considered our brand history (origin), identified the problem we solve (consumer) and understood the tone of our voice (archetype). We've also seen examples of how other brands have tackled these concepts. Now we have the tools to put this all together and start drafting our purpose statements.

Writing purpose statements is hard and takes time. Even the best brands revisit and revise.

For example, for the past 45 years, Patagonia's purpose has been to "build the best product, cause no unnecessary harm, use business to inspire and implement solutions to the environmental crisis."

While this has served them well, in the past few years, Patagonia has expanded its clothing offerings and doubled down on its sustainability initiatives, including investing in sustainable startups and launching an activist hub to connect its consumers directly with grassroots environmental organizations. In 2018, in response to expected tax cuts, CEO Rose Marcario announced the company would donate $10 million to environmental organizations.

When it comes to living out a Purpose Advantage, Patagonia has been supreme. But even they understood the evolution — the necessary evolution — every brand must face. Because while they originally emphasized causing no harm to the environment, they now (as of December 2018) are moving from a reactive approach to a proactive initiative to save the earth.

In fact, their new purpose statement reads "Patagonia is in business to save our home planet." The new statement is clear, active and urgent — a necessary change to reflect the values of their consumers. As cultural conversation shifted to discuss the crisis that is climate change, Patagonia was ready to join, and lead, the conversation.

Whatever is relevant now may not be so in five years. The key with your purpose statement is to get as clear as possible on a purpose that resonates with you, your consumer, and cultural needs and conversations, fully expecting to evolve as needed.

For this module, discuss Patagonia and their evolution and prepare to draft your purpose statement. While there is no formula, a good starting point is as follows:

We (Brand) [do/provide/create _____ /what the brand is good at], so/in order that [people/others/the world] can [what the brand's products/service etc. enables].

ACTIVITY

one

Using the answers from the earlier frameworks, answer the following:

What is my brand good at:

_____

_____

_____

_____

People we serve:

_____

_____

_____

_____

Higher purpose our product/service enables:

_____

_____

_____

two   Considering the tone of your selected archetype and the answer above, write your purpose statement.

three   Does your statement check the box on the following?

Authentic: Does this feel true to our brand?

Need: Does it solve a problem or fulfill a societal need?

Growth: Is there potential for business growth?

Inspiration: Does this have the potential to inspire, inside and outside the business?

_____

_____

_____

_____

_____

Different: Does this feel different to what's already on the market?

_____

_____

_____

_____

_____

PROOF PLAN™

INSIDE EXERCISE

GUIDING QUESTION

What are the actions you
will take inside the company
that will bring your purpose
to life?

"Brand purpose is foundational. You can't just
say you have a brand purpose, you have to put
meat on the bone behind it, not only talking
about it externally but delivering on it
internally within your company and ultimately
with the customer."

Denise Karkos
CMO at TD Ameritrade®

Now that you have a draft brand purpose, can you cite ways in which your company culture already supports this purpose? Can we truly live out the purpose (i.e. avoid a Starbucks' "Race Together")? Are there any other ideas you have that you should start, stop or continue across how your workforce is structured, incentivized and engaged?

ACTIVITY

Prove your purpose with internal audiences. Using your purpose statement, document ways your existing company culture supports your purpose and ideate on new ideas covering your:

one   Organization and work groups

two   Workforce compensation, benefits and incentives

_____

_____

_____

_____

_____

three   Employee engagement and communication

_____

_____

_____

_____

_____

four   Office visual cues

PROOF PLAN™
OUTSIDE EXERCISE

GUIDING QUESTION

What are the actions you will take outside the company, externally, that will bring your purpose to life?

With a clearer purpose in place, it's time to do your homework on the impact of your purpose. If your purpose is touching on something even remotely controversial, whether it be tied to differing beliefs, strategies or outcomes, it's important to analyze the impacts of your decision to own your part of the conversation. How can you bring your purpose to life outside the business through product, experience, design and communication?

For example, Seventh Generation realized early on that just making safer, more effective cleaning products wasn't enough. In order to really hit their goal of protecting life for the next seven generations, they would be engaging in bigger conversations about the environment, government policy and manufacturing standards. By completing their due diligence early, leadership took a holistic approach to viewing all the ways their involvement could breed both tension and opportunities.

In response to the widening conversation, Seventh Generation installed departments devoted to lobbying for better legislation regarding labeling products. They made innovating their product packaging a top priority. They understand the impact of the promise they were making to themselves and their consumers and prepared accordingly.

Your brand should recognize the impact of even the most well-intentioned move. If part of your plan involves changing the way your product is packaged, investigate the impact on stakeholders. Will the consumer ultimately receive an inferior product? While the packaging is recyclable, is it obvious to the consumer? How will the change in packaging materials impact margins?

In this workshop, consider sharing Seventh Generation's example or the cautionary tale of Gillette's The Best a Man Can Be campaign®.

The campaign, which was launched in early 2019, caused their net sentiment as measured by Intermark using NetBase, to drop from a net 65 percent positive commentary to 14 percent negative, a 79-point drop, in less than 30 days.

To discuss the mixed reactions and obvious displeasure with the campaign, I asked Jake McKenzie, CEO of Intermark Group, to weigh in on where he believed the brand stumbled.

GILLETTE'S THE BEST A MAN CAN BE®

The centerpiece of the campaign was a short film of less than two minutes that replaced Gillette's famous slogan, "the best a man can get," with "the best a man can be" while portraying and condemning instances of bullying, aggressive behavior, sexism and sexual harassment. Along with the video, Gillette® launched a website where the company pledged to distribute $1 million per year for the next three years to non-profit organizations executing the most interesting and impactful projects designed to help men of all ages achieve their personal best.

According to Jake, after a few years of having their market share eroded by cheaper delivery alternatives, Gillette was forced to change tactics. Until then, Gillette's product messaging focused mostly on the quality of the product. In fact, the very slogan — the best a man can get — spoke directly to their core brand claim of having a technically superior product. However, users began to see razors as more of a commodity and were pushing back against the cost of the replacement blades, driving intense competition. Adding to that competitive pressure was the fact that the market for razors had plateaued and was not projected to grow. The culmination of competition and a stagnant market led to the somewhat inevitable change in tactics.

Advertising prior to internal and external action is a #Fail

Author's quote

The change in tactics was an answer not only to the change in competition, but a rightful understanding by Gillette that younger consumers are looking for brands with a voice. Nike had recently seen great success in their campaign with Colin Kaepernick, to the tune of a $6 billion increase in overall value, even amidst mixed reactions and a boycott. It's understandable why Gillette believed joining in on the conversation surrounded misogyny, sexism, and toxic masculinity was a sound decision. But unfortunately, while the strategy for the Gillette ad was correct, their execution lacked foresight.

For starters, Gillette lacked the authority to speak on sexism, not because they don't serve the female and male market, but because they historically haven't served them *equally*.

Gillette is one of many consumer brands that charge female consumers more for products designed for their gender (pink razors, for example). Known as the Pink Tax, this practice created a dissonance between what they're saying, "We are against sexism!", and what they're doing — charging women more for a comparable product in a pastel color.

Next, Gillette's final two-minute ad ran into some rough spots in the editing process. What was supposed to be a short clip of dads discouraging their sons from resolving conflict with violence instead played out as a father discouraging his son from roughhousing with another boy. While about half of Gillette's audience understood the call to resist violence, the other half felt young boys playing in the backyard wasn't a sign of violence or toxic masculinity. In Jake's words, "Gillette failed to identify a universally agreed-upon evil."

Lastly, Gillette made a huge error by including themselves as a solution to a problem before any real action had been taken. Kicking-off the campaign by taking credit for their positive actions left consumers underwhelmed and a little disappointed.

NIKE'S 30TH ANNIVERSARY JUST DO IT® CAMPAIGN

Announced in late 2018, Nike's campaign featured former NFL quarterback Colin Kaepernick as the masthead for the commentary on current social issues. The commercials and print ads included pictures of Kaepernick (who had received much conversation regarding his decision to kneel during the national anthem to draw attention to police brutality) and focused on the message, "believe in something, even if it means sacrificing everything."

ACTIVITY

Prove your purpose to an external audience. Using your purpose statement, ideate on how it might impact your:

one   *Product:* How could the way you design and make your
           product change?

_____

_____

_____

_____

_____

two   *Consumer Experience:* How would this affect ease of use
           and brand?

_____

_____

_____

_____

_____

three   *Design:* How would this affect visibility, packaging, location?

_____

_____

_____

_____

_____

four   *Communication:* How would this affect storytelling, narratives and activations?

_____

_____

_____

_____

_____

PROOF PLAN™
MEASURE EXERCISE

GUIDING QUESTION

What are the indicators
that are relevant to
living your purpose?

"A principle isn't a principle until it costs you money," said Bill Bernbach, founder of advertising agency DDB, who famously refused to work on cigarette advertising after the General Surgeon warning against smoking in 1964. In this exercise, we discuss the measurable action of your purpose. If you are living your purpose, what are the things that you won't do?

In business, what gets measured gets improved — we can thank Peter Drucker for that gem. With purpose-driven businesses or brands adopting a Purpose Advantage, this holds doubly true. If your purpose is to put people first, you will have to get clear on how that's measured, not only to indicate improvement, but to establish rewards and incentives for your teams and employees.

By connecting your purpose not just to profits, but to rewards, all employees will see the outcome of their actions. For this workshop, considering sharing stories of how companies are already doing this.

For example, at Seventh Generation, 20 percent of their annual bonus is based on their success at delivering on their sustainability and advocacy targets. Not only is the purpose measured, but then it is rewarded. For Joey Bergstein, "We put our money where our mouth is. We have goals timed to accomplish by 2025."

During our conversations, Joey shared one of his proudest, but most difficult, experiences as CEO.

Early in 2012, Tide released Tide Pods. These small dissolvable pods quickly struck a nerve with consumers and became an increasingly popular laundry solution. At Seventh Generation, the concept of a detergent pod made perfect sense; the pods used less packaging, minimal water, and had a smaller carbon footprint.

However, while the research and development department was out creating Seventh Generations version of the Tide Pod, news broke of consumers — mainly children — mistaking the brightly colored packages for candy and ingesting the pods, resulting in poisoning and in some cases, death. Between 2011 and 2013, the number of annual emergency department visits for all laundry detergent-related injuries for young children more than tripled, from 2,862 to 9,004.[14]

In response, Joey and his team brought in a third-party company to conduct tests on their detergent pods to determine toxicity if ingested. The third-party company confirmed that individually, each ingredient was non-toxic if consumed. However, given they do not test on living creatures, they could not confirm safety when the ingredients were ingested together.

This left Joey and his team in an interesting position. Technically, they'd done their due diligence, but because rewards were framed around their impact on the seven generations, Joey and his team ultimately shelved the detergent pods in favor of a powdered version that was confirmed to be safe.

While Joey admitted it was impossible to know if the liquid version would have performed better, he felt confident his team had made the right decision. They chose safety for people before profits, not only because it was the right thing to do, but because that was what would be ultimately rewarded.

ACTIVITY

Prove your purpose through measurement. Ideate on:

one   What would be an indicator that would measure how your putting your purpose to work through action (e.g. number of people positively impacted by your actions, change in behavior, reduction in environmental emissions)?

_____

_____

_____

_____

_____

two   Examples of what your not going to do in support of your purpose.

_____

_____

_____

_____

three   How would you measure the impact of your purpose on the business (e.g. increase in sales, brand reputation and loyalty, reduction in costs, increase in employee engagement & retention, increase in innovation, stronger supplier relationships)?

THE PITCH EXERCISE

GUIDING QUESTION

What are the next steps you need to take?

Notice this exercise is not "market, market, market!" This isn't because marketing should be excluded from the Purpose Advantage, but because understanding when to communicate your actions to your consumers is a delicate decision. Even with the perfect purpose grounded in strong research, understanding the nuances of when and how your brand should begin to take credit is unique to each brand.

For this exercise, share the following example from MOD Pizza to fuel the discussion.

For MOD Pizza, they take credit for their purpose only by hinting at it in their messaging. "We believe in second chances" only becomes a call out to their hiring process when consumers visit their website to learn more about the company mission. The subtlety is strategic for MOD. According to co-founder Scott Svenson:

"Because we are so sincere and committed to the purpose, we don't want to taint it by trying to leverage it from a marketing perspective. We tease it out a little bit." Scott shared a saying used in stores that goes, "We make pizza to serve people." Scott and his team call it "Spreading MODness."

For Scott, the goal is to "elicit a conversation between a customer and a MOD Squadder because there is no one better to tell the MOD story than a MOD Squadder who's felt the impact of MOD."

MOD continues to be very careful about how it shares its purpose, with the goal that over time, "people start to realize that the experience they're having in our stores has a depth and an energy to it that they don't get elsewhere," says Scott.

This isn't to say you can't be direct with your consumers. Instead, be sensitive to touchpoints and when the consumer will be most open to not only recognizing your actions, but rewarding you for them.

Aline Santos, Unilever's EVP of Global Marketing put it this way:

"What the research shows is that, providing you are honest about what you are doing and that you have a plan to grow, people are prepared to go with you. That's better than not talking at all because you don't think the numbers are big enough. People like to be taken with you on the journey, not told about it afterwards. If you do have a problem or need to alter direction, providing you maintain an open and continuous dialogue, people accept it and even admire your efforts all the more, because they know this isn't easy and it shows humanity in the way the brand is managed."[15]

ACTIVITY

An elevator pitch is a short description of your idea that will engage your audience. Based on your top ideas from previous exercises, write how you would share the following in two minutes or less:

one   Your organization's purpose.

two   How you prove your commitment inside your organization with employees.

three   How you prove your commitment outside your organization with consumers.

_____

_____

_____

_____

_____

four   How your organization holds itself accountable.

_____

_____

_____

_____

_____

9   "2017 Cone Communications CSR Study" Cone, 17 May 2017,
    http://www.conecomm.com/2017-cone-communications-csr-study-pdf

10 Sustainable Development Goals" United Nations, 24 July 2018,
    https://sustainabledevelopment.un.org/sdgs

11 "Our History" Unilever.com, 2019, https://www.unilever.com/about/who-we-are/our-history/

12 Mark, M., & Pearson, C. S. (2002). *The Hero and the Outlaw: Building Extraordinary Brands Through the Power of Archetypes.* New York: McGraw-Hill.

13 Hartwell, M., & Chen, J. C. (2012). *Archetypes in Branding: A Toolkit for Creatives and Strategists.* Cincinnati: F W Media.

14 Meth, Jake, "The Tragic Side of Tide Pods" Fortune.com, 19 February 2019,
    http://fortune.com/longform/tide-pod-poisoning-injuries-epidemic/

15 "Making Purpose Pay: Inspiring Sustainable Living" Unilever.com, 2018,
    https://www.unilever.com/Images/making-purpose-pay-inspiring-sustainable-living-170515_tcm244-506419_en.pdf

NINE

Where Do We Go From Here?

Throughout the entire Purpose Advantage process, the underlying theme has been to embed purpose within your company to ensure that at each touchpoint your consumers understand what they're paying for, especially when it includes a social good. While this book does distill it down to four frameworks, it's important to note, this isn't a simple or fast process, but an ongoing commitment to delivering on your purpose.

Your company purpose and the way you go about executing it will evolve. It's not a one-stop shop or a one-time action, but a continued commitment to instilling your Purpose Advantage.

While this book focuses on mature brands, look out for future work addressing additional advantages available to your brand. The modern consumer is always shifting and sending out signals on where they are headed next. My job over the next few years will be to take those signals and create actionable steps for you.

Until then, I look forward to hearing from you and how your Purpose Advantage is taking shape. Good news, bad news, or otherwise, please share your experiences with me at *jfromm@barkleyus.com*.

I encourage you to look a little deeper the next time you take a stroll down the detergent aisle or when you grab your next pizza. The Purpose Advantage™ is all around us. As more and more brands step up to take their slice, make sure you don't get left empty-handed.

You know that one last thing before you're out the door, the quick glance in the mirror—a simple reflection, and then it's off to make your work mean as much as it can in the world? Take a moment to ask and answer: **What's my personal purpose?**

_____

_____

_____

_____

_____

_____

_____

WHAT'S MY PERSONAL PURPOSE?

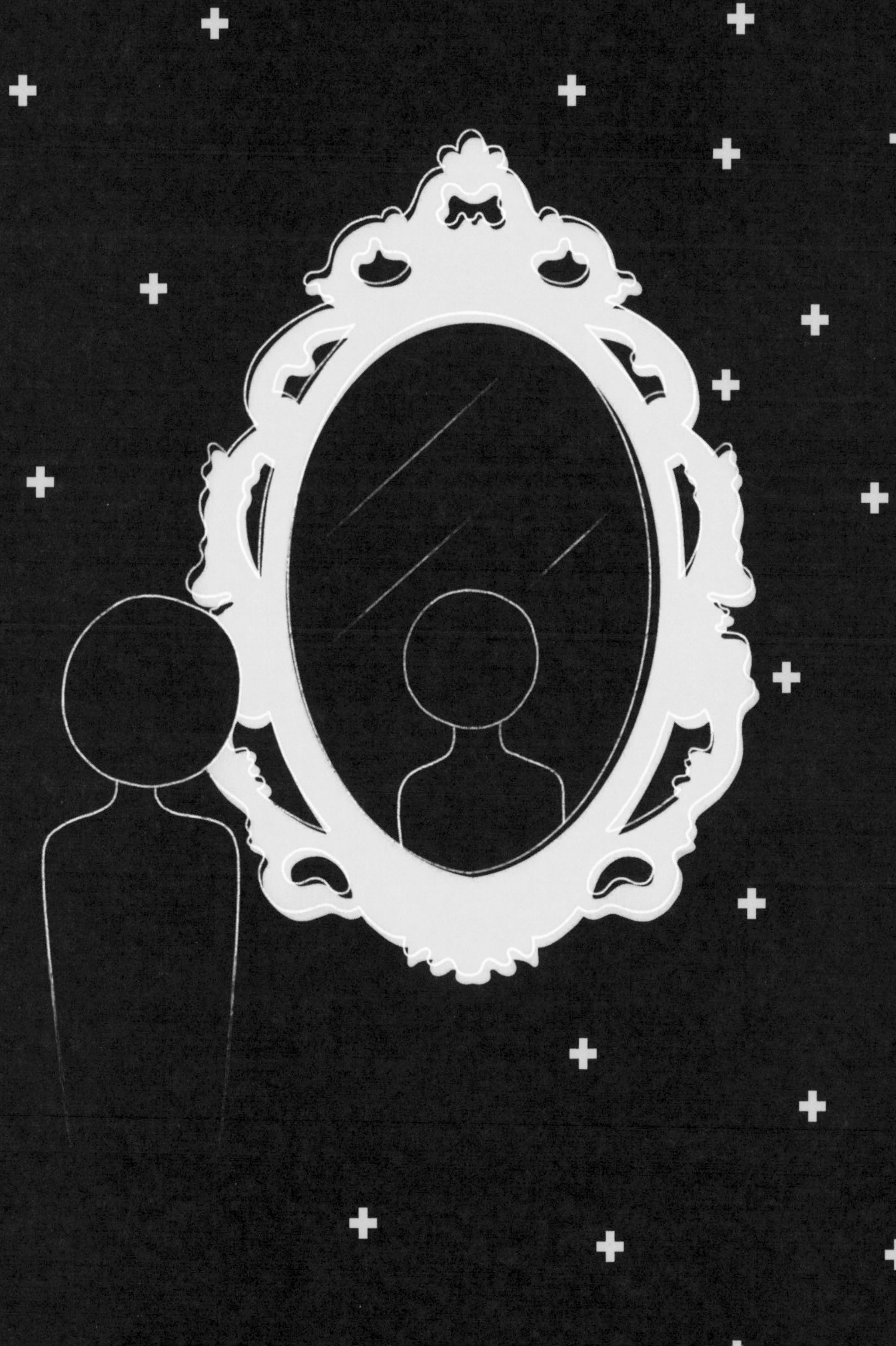

REFERENCES

1 "Inside Seventh Generation's Quest to Blow Up Without Selling Out" Fortune, 2016,
http://fortune.com/seventh-generation-green-cleaning-products/

2 "Sales share of the leading 10 liquid laundry detergent brands of the United States in 2018"
Statista.com, 2018, https://www.statista.com/statistics/251472/sales-share-of-the-leading-10-
liquid-laundry-detergent-brands-of-the-us/

3 "Making Purpose Pay: Inspiring Sustainable Living" Unilever.com, 2018,
https://www.unilever.com/Images/making-purpose-pay-inspiring-sustainable-living-170515_
tcm244-506419_en.pdf

4 "Porter Novelli/Cone Purpose Premium Index" Cone Communications, 13 November 2018,
http://www.conecomm.com/research-blog/purpose-premium

5 Fink, Larry, "Purpose & Profit" Letter to CEOs, 17 January 2019,
https://www.blackrock.com/corporate/investor-relations/larry-fink-ceo-letter

6 "2017 Cone Communications CSR Study" Cone, 17 May 2017,
http://www.conecomm.com/2017-cone-communications-csr-study-pdf

7 Announcing the Dove Real Beauty Pledge. (17, June 13). Retrieved June 17, 19, from
https://www.unilever.com/news/news-and-features/Feature-article/2017/Announcing-the-
Dove-Real-Beauty-Pledge.html

8 Reed, Russel, "One -for-Non: Aid Dependency and the 'TOMS Model'", Harvard Political
Review, 22 March 2017, http://harvardpolitics.com/world/one-for-none/

9 "2017 Cone Communications CSR Study" Cone, 17 May 2017,
http://www.conecomm.com/2017-cone-communications-csr-study-pdf

10 "Sustainable Development Goals" United Nations, 24 July 2018,
https://sustainabledevelopment.un.org/sdgs

11 "Our History" Unilever.com, 2019, https://www.unilever.com/about/who-we-are/our-history/

12 Mark, M., & Pearson, C. S. (2002). *The Hero and the Outlaw: Building Extraordinary Brands
Through the Power of Archetypes.* New York: McGraw-Hill.

13 Hartwell, M., & Chen, J. C. (2012). *Archetypes in Branding: A Toolkit for Creatives and
Strategists.* Cincinnati: F W Media.

14 Meth, Jake, "The Tragic Side of Tide Pods" Fortune.com, 19 February 2019,
http://fortune.com/longform/tide-pod-poisoning-injuries-epidemic/

15 "Making Purpose Pay: Inspiring Sustainable Living" Unilever.com, 2018,
https://www.unilever.com/Images/making-purpose-pay-inspiring-sustainable-living-170515_
tcm244-506419_en.pdf

A

B

✚ JEFF FROMM ✚

As one of the world's leading consumer trend experts, Jeff Fromm is a contributor to Forbes and a co-author of three prior books on Millennials and Gen Z. His initial book was the result of the first large-scale public study of Millennials as consumers, conducted in a research partnership between Barkley, Boston Consulting Group and Service Management Group in 2010 & 2011.

When he's not on an airplane, he works as a partner at ad agency Barkley, leading workshops, speaking and consulting with executives. Jeff also serves on the Board of Directors for Three Dog Bakery and has a rescue dog named Winnie.

Jeff graduated from the Wharton School of the University of Pennsylvania and attended the London School of Economics.

jefffromm.com | barkleyus.com | linkedin@jefffromm